The ABC of Wealth

The How of Genuine Wealth

Andrew Bawa

The ABC of Wealth by Andrew Bawa. —1st edition. ISBN
978-1-9994837-5-3

Publisher: Younik Publishing
Ordering Information:
Quantity sales. Special discounts are available on quantity
purchases by corporations, associations, and others. For details,
contact the Special Sales Department" at the address above.

Table of Contents

Acknowledgements

I would like to thank my family for their love and support. My amazing fiancee, Emem Ukpong, my children, Elnessa and Elswidih. Thank you for being patient with me, supporting me and cheering me on.

I would also like to appreciate the NextGen Office Staff, OgheneKefe Aomreore, Toluwalope Dare, Toni Ann Samuda and Benjamin Ozore as well as Theresa & Emeka Ogueri of The Younik Publishing team who all worked tirelessly to make this project a success.

I would also like to express my heartfelt gratitude to the NextGen Worship Centre family for their love.

Introduction

You are not created to be poor.

I know that may come as a surprise to you, especially if you have been acquainted with the Christian community as it is a common belief in many Christian circles that wealth is evil.

You may have heard or have been taught phrases such as "money is the root of all evil", or "it is difficult for a wealthy person to enter the gates of heaven". Unbeknownst to you, this may be the message you have internalized about wealth. This could be what you believe about wealth unconsciously.

Wealth is Spiritual

Unfortunately, the most ignorant set of people in matters of wealth are believers. We are so heavenly-minded that we become earthly irrelevant. We forget that we can't achieve what we don't understand, and many of us have never taken the time to study, learn or even pray about wealth.

Wealth is spiritual. In order to succeed in the area of wealth, you need to understand the spiritual dynamics of wealth.

Nobody succeeds financially without the power of the spirit. Now depending on the person, some rely on evil spirits while you and I should rely on the Holy Spirit.

Let's take the Israelites, for example, after many years of slavery in Egypt God finally heard their complaints and sent them Moses, the deliverer. In Exodus 3, God gave Moses instructions on what the Israelites should do as they leave Egypt.

Exodus 3:21-22 (NLT)
And I will cause the Egyptians to look favourably on you. They will give you gifts when you go so you will not leave empty-handed. 22 Every Israelite woman will ask for articles of silver and gold and fine clothing from her Egyptian neighbours and from the foreign women in their houses. You will dress your sons and daughters with these, stripping the Egyptians of their wealth."

I wonder what the Israelites were thinking when they heard those instructions. I can imagine the Israelite women scoffing at the thought that their slave masters and mistresses would actually just give them all their gold jewelry just because they asked!

Would you give someone your employee or your neighbour your favourite clothes and most valued jewelry if they randomly ask you? Some of you would not even give your family members, let alone a stranger.

But because wealth is spiritual, the Egyptians released their wealth to the Israelites without any struggle or complaints. They simply obeyed and followed God's instructions.

Have you ever wondered why you would always go to some restaurants or some stores even if they have horrible customer service or they are completely out of your way? Have you ever seen some foreign gods at the locations of some businesses that you patronize?

Most times, these people have paid a price or sacrificed to their gods so that their businesses are patronized. They have made an agreement on how much they want to sell on that day and no matter what, they will reach those numbers.

This is why sometimes in the middle of the night you are just suddenly craving a random thing from that restaurant, you order it and have it delivered to you only for you to take one bite and discard it for a later day. That is because they paid a price to their gods and requested that a particular amount of money has to be made that day and you spent your money for them to reach their sales for the day.

Wealth is spiritual.

Wealth also answers to sacrifice. Every wealthy person has sacrificed something to reach where they are. Unfortunately, many believers do not want to make any sacrifices or pay the price of what they desire, they just want it to be delivered to them on a silver platter.

The people of the world will go to herbalists, demons, and the spirit of darkness to conjure the gods of this world to give them money. But we go to our Father who has the whole world in His hands. Silver and gold are His and everything on earth belongs to Him.

1 Chronicles 29:12 (NLT)

Wealth and honour come from you alone, for you rule over everything. Power and might are in your hand, and at your discretion, people are made great and given strength.

This means that, instead of spending all your time and energy seeking money, spend it seeking God, who is the owner of all things and the giver of all things. In Him lies everything you are looking for and more.

This will be the main focus of this book. Now that you know that wealth is spiritual and that it can only come from God, I will show you further how to access this wealth from our Father. I will show you the scriptural principles of wealth as well as the practical applications of these principles.

Beyond that, this book will also outline the physical channels of wealth. It will answer questions such as, what can I do now to be wealthy? How can I understand the systems in the country I live in and how can I use those systems to my advantage?

You are in for a great treat and I am so happy that you are investing in yourself and taking this important first step on the road to being wealthy. Knowledge is great, but applied knowledge is what will bring you results.

Reading this book is a great first step, but applying the principles you learn within will benefit you most. Please do your best to practice everything you learn in this book. I cannot wait to hear all your testimonies!

Chapter 1

Holiness

Experts often say that to change your life, you must change your mind. At the core of who you are, what you believe and every decision you make are thoughts and experiences that have been buried in your subconscious.

What you currently believe about wealth is because of what you know from experience. Maybe you are among the few that grew up with the idea that "money does not grow on trees" repeatedly told to you by the adults in your life. You most likely believe that money is difficult to make or difficult to attain.

Or maybe you're on the opposite end of the spectrum, nothing was denied to you by your family. You understand that money is a tool that is easily available to use when needed. You most likely believe that wealth is easily attainable for you.

Or maybe you are somewhere in between these two extremes.

Whatever your case may be, we can agree that to get to where you want to be and attain genuine wealth you have to deal with your foundation.

The Foundation of Genuine Wealth

We have already established that wealth is spiritual and that it can only come from God. So why have you not been able to attain it yet?

To answer that, we will start with the foundation of genuine wealth. If wealth is spiritual then the only foundation you need is holiness.

Holiness is the key and the basic foundation of genuine wealth. I know when you think about holiness all you think about is thou must not do this and that, you are right, we are instructed to be holy. However, it is more than that.

2 Timothy 2:19 (NLT)
But God's truth stands firm like a foundation stone with this inscription: "The Lord knows

those who are his," and "All who belong to the Lord must turn away from evil."

Until the foundation is right, nothing lasting can be built upon it. If you already know the principles of wealth but your foundation is wrong, you will still end up with the same results.

As a believer, righteousness is imputed to you by the finished work of Christ but holiness is your own responsibility.

To understand this better, let us go back to the very beginning where we first saw genuine wealth; the garden of Eden.

In the garden, man was in a place where everything was made available to him, nothing was missing, nothing was broken, and he had everything that he needed. That is genuine wealth, which we can see is God's original intention and design for mankind.

The word "Eden" means presence. That means that before anything else, man was supposed to live in the presence of God. In the presence of God is where he found health, peace, provision, companionship, a spouse, shelter, and everything else that he needed. That is genuine, all-around wealth. Man was not intended to lack anything.

After man sinned and was removed from the garden (removed from the presence), he never again went back to the same quality of life he had previously. That was when toiling started, that was the beginning of the "hustle," as we call it nowadays.

Man moved from abundance to lack, from prosperity to poverty, and from plenty to penury all because he SINNED! Sin is the one thing that can take us away from the presence (Eden) of God and we already know that being away from the presence of God is being away from wealth.

The only way to stay in the presence of God, which is where wealth is found, is by remaining holy and being consecrated to God.

The good news is that there is a solution! God knew that we can not obtain holiness with our own effort. And so He found a way for us to be reconciled back to him through our faith in the finished work of Christ.

God sent his only son to die for us so that whoever believes in him can have eternal life and be made holy as He originally intended. We can now confidently step back into God's presence where we can find genuine wealth.

Psalms 16:11 (AMP)
*You will show me the path of life;
In your presence is fullness of joy;
At your right hand are pleasures
forevermore*

If you have not yet experienced the transformational power of Christ's resurrection I would like to invite you to take this journey with me. There is nothing we can do on our own to allow us access to God's presence, only Jesus can do that. He is the way to the Father.

If you are ready to make the decision to accept Jesus as your saviour and through him access the presence of God, I invite you to say this short prayer with me:

Dear God, I know that I am a sinner and there is nothing that I can do to save myself. I confess my complete helplessness to forgive my own sin or to work my way to heaven. At this moment I trust Christ alone as the One who took my sin when He died on the cross. I believe that He did all that will ever be necessary for me to stand in your holy presence.

Therefore, I accept and acknowledge Jesus Christ as my Lord and Saviour. I receive the gift of salvation through faith. Thank you for making me yours. From now on, help me to live for you through the power of the Holy Spirit. In Jesus' precious name, I pray. Amen.

Congratulations on making the best decision of your life. If you have said this prayer and would like to connect with me, please send me an email or reach out to me on my social platforms. Welcome to the family of God!

The Case Study of Job

The story of Job is one of the most interesting stories in the Bible. Job was a very wealthy man in his community, in fact, the scriptures said he was "the richest man in that area" (Job 1:3).

Beyond his wealth, the scriptures describe Job as a blameless man who had integrity, feared God, and kept away from evil (Job 1:1). In short, he was the ideal man; a great relationship with God, an amazing family, and great wealth.

However, Job faced unimaginable loss, not only of his possessions but also of all his offspring and a deterioration of his health. Can you imagine what that must have felt like?

After serving God and walking blamelessly before Him, Job lost everything. It takes great faith and trust n God to come back from a loss like that. Fortunately, Job did not curse God throughout his predicament He understood that wealth is spiritual and it only comes from the living God.

Job 22:23-25 (NLT)
If you return to the Almighty, you will be restored—
so clean up your life.
If you give up your lust for money
and throw your precious gold into the river,

the Almighty himself will be your treasure.
He will be your precious silver!

The key is returning back to his presence, until you step out of iniquity you can't step into prosperity. It is one thing to have wealth and a completely different thing to enjoy that wealth.

We know of or have heard of many wealthy individuals who are struggling with health concerns. There are others who are struggling with their family relationships, their marriages, or even their mental health. No matter how much money you have, some things can't be bought.

This is why the Bible says that the blessing of the Lord makes rich and adds no sorrow to it (Proverbs 10:22). His blessing is all-rounded, it goes beyond just money but includes your health, your family, and your safety among other things.

When you really study the wealthy people in scripture, you will see that the circumstances around them did not stop God's blessing in their life. Isaac for example lived in a famine-ridden land. When everyone around him was running off in search of greener pastures, God asked him to sow right where he was.

I can imagine his neighbours mocking him and laughing at him for "wasting" precious seeds in famine. But Isaac was not concerned with all of that, he sowed as he was instructed and scripture says he reaped a hundredfold!

Genesis 26:12-13 (NLT)
"When Isaac planted his crops that year, he harvested a hundred times more grain than he planted, for the Lord blessed him. 13 He became a very rich man, and his wealth continued to grow.

The blessing of the Lord is what makes the difference, but you can not obtain this blessing without being in His presence. And you can not be in His presence without holiness.

Why Do Sinners Prosper?

After the conversation about wealth being spiritual and how holiness is the key to wealth, you probably can't help but ask why sinners prosper. That is an excellent question and luckily, we are not the only ones who have asked this.

King David asked this very question in Psalms 73. He did not understand why sinners seem to get away with being evil and mocking God, and yet still enjoy riches and prosperity. In fact, David questioned why he was keeping himself pure and holy if all he gets is trouble.

Psalms 73:13-14 (NLT)
Did I keep my heart pure for nothing?
Did I keep myself innocent for no reason?
I get nothing but trouble all day long;
every morning brings me pain.

Have you ever felt like David? Have you wondered why you bother living a committed and submitted life to God while those who don't seem to be doing so much better than you? Maybe your colleagues who steal from work mock you for being so "sanctimonious". Their accounts are getting fatter while you can't afford your basic needs. Maybe you have considered joining them in their evil deeds but the Holy Spirit nudges you to choose holiness and not escape the presence of God.

God in his wisdom responds to David and caused him to understand that the prosperity of the wicked is actually the bait of satan. It leads them on a slippery slope and causes them to think that they are self-made and they can do without God.

Psalms 73:16-20 (NLT)
So I tried to understand why the wicked prosper.
But what a difficult task it is!
Then I went into your sanctuary, O God,
and I finally understood the destiny of the wicked.
Truly, you put them on a slippery path
and send them sliding over the cliff to destruction.
In an instant they are destroyed,
completely swept away by terrors.
When you arise, O Lord,
you will laugh at their silly ideas
as a person laughs at dreams in the morning.

No matter what it looks like on the outside, nothing else matters more than being in the right standing with God. True wealth is not just about money, it encompasses your health, peace, joy, safety, and most importantly, your place in eternity.

Yes, wealth is spiritual, so this means that you can either get it from God or from the devil. But if the devil gives you wealth, then sorrow is definitely attached to it. Some people want wealth at all costs and they are willing to bow to the enemy to get it. However, the repercussions of this decision are heavy. They are not worth your soul.

We know that getting anything from the devil will require you to bow to him. He is very skilled at enticing you with get-rich-quick schemes and easy ways out. A good example is when he attempted to make Jesus bow to him with the promise of giving him all the kingdoms of the world and their glory (Matthew 4:8-9).

Nothing should entice you to forget your place in the kingdom of God. That is why God reminds us in Proverbs 1:10 that when sinners entice you, do not consent. Anything you get out of the presence of God you will need to remain out of the presence of God to keep it. Nothing you get out of God's presence is worth your soul.

Mark 8:36 (NLT)
And what do you benefit if you gain the whole world but lose your own soul?

The Case Study of the Israelites

In the first chapter, we saw how the Israelites were delivered from Egypt but they did not leave empty-handed. God granted them favour before their Egyptian masters and allowed the Israelites to spoil them; they left with their silver, gold, and fine clothing.

However, when you read further along in the book of Exodus, you see the Israelites stuck in the wilderness and struggling with poverty. They did not even have enough to eat and were constantly complaining to Moses. They even thought of returning back to Egypt, their place of bondage.

Isn't it ironic? That in the wilderness, they thought of going back to that same place of pain and bondage even though they were on their way to a much better place of abundance?

God had promised the Israelites when they were leaving Egypt that they are going to Canaan, a land filled with milk and honey; a place of abundance. In Egypt, the Israelites experienced so much pain and suffering to the extent that they cried out to God for help and for deliverance.

God had promised them victory and had delivered them from their bondage with great signs and wonders, but the Israelites still refused to believe and ended up in sin, complaining, murmuring, and grumbling against the Lord and his servants. As a result, they spent 40 years wandering in the desert and God made sure that everyone who had sinned against him does not make it into the promised land.

5 Sins that Stopped the Israelites from Possessing the Land

1. Lust

To lust means to have a very strong desire for something. In this case, the Israelites lusted after what God does not want for them. They lusted after meat. God had been providing manna for them to eat in the desert but at some point, they started craving meat.
Their craving for meat caused them to complain and wish that they were back in Egypt, where God delivered them after years of crying out to Him.

Numbers 11:4-6 (NKJV)
Now the mixed multitude who were among them yielded to intense craving; so the children of Israel also wept again and said: "Who will give us meat to eat? We remember the fish which we ate freely in Egypt, the cucumbers, the melons, the leeks, the onions, and the garlic; but now our whole being is dried up; there is nothing at all except this manna before our eyes!"

Eventually, God gave them the meat they so desired but while they were still eating it, he sent a plague to consume them!

Be careful what you crave and desire. Be sure that you do not desire what God does not desire for you. As we can see from the Israelites, the lust of the flesh can cause you not to live in the abundance you were promised. Lust takes you away from God's presence which takes you away from genuine wealth.

2. Unbelief, Complaining, and Murmuring

When you read through the Israelites' journey from Egypt to the promised land, you can not miss the frequency with which they complain about everything. They complained when they were in bondage, they complained when they were about to cross the Red Sea, they complained about what to eat, they complained about Moses and his leadership, and they complained when they were asked to survey the land before taking possession of it, they just kept complaining.

They did not believe in God's promise even though they had experienced God's power in many ways in the past. From the Egyptian plagues to parting the red sea and even receiving manna from heaven, you can not deny the magnitude of the manifestation of God's power in their lives. But yet, they still lived in unbelief.

The Israelites failed to believe in the God who had revealed himself to them so often. They had experienced his manifest presence and power but they still refused to believe in him.

Numbers 14:11 (NLT)
And the Lord said to Moses, "How long will these people treat me with contempt? Will they never believe me, even after all the miraculous signs I have done among them?

Unbelief is one of the ways you can lose your promise.

3. Sexual Immorality

The sin of sexual immorality has been around for a long time. In the Old Testament, we read about many instances of sexual immorality, from fornication to rape, prostitution, adultery, and even incest. Sexual immorality is not new and not limited to our current generation.

The Bible speaks about this sin as the only sin you can commit against your body. You can't pray against sexual immorality, Paul in 1st Corinthians 6:18 advises us to flee from it. When you are faced with a temptation, instead of thinking you are strong enough to handle it, flee!

In Numbers 25, we see that the Israelites committed sexual immorality with some Moabite women. This led to God killing 24,000 of them by plague. Their immorality cost them their lives.

Now, because of their sexual immorality, we see that the Israelites committed idolatry. They not only performed sexual sin but their sexual sin also led them to worship other gods, which is the next sin we will be discussing.

Numbers 25:1-3 (NIV)
While Israel was staying in Shittim, the men began to indulge in sexual immorality with Moabite women, who invited them to the sacrifices to their gods. The people ate the sacrificial meal and bowed down before these gods. So Israel yoked themselves to the Baal of Peor. And the Lord's anger burned against them.

Verse 3 says that they yoked themselves to the Baal of Peor. They yoked themselves to a foreign god because they yoked themselves to the Moabite women in sexual sin. It is not worth it to defile your body and sin against God for just a few minutes of pleasure. If you desire to partake in God's promise of wealth, be sure to stay away from sexual sin. It may cost you your life.

4. Idolatry

Idolatry simply means the worship of idols. To explain further, it means worshipping something or someone as though it were God. As we saw in the example above, 24,000 men were killed by a plague because they bowed down to Baal, who was a foreign god. The word of God is clear regarding the worship of other gods.

Exodus 20:3-5 (NLT)
*You must not have any other god but me.
"You must not make for yourself an idol of
any kind or an image of anything in the
heavens or on the earth or in the sea. You
must not bow down to them or worship
them, for I, the Lord your God, am a jealous
God who will not tolerate your affection for
any other gods. I lay the sins of the parents
upon their children; the entire family is
affected—even children in the third and
fourth generations of those who reject me.*

This is the commandment that God gave us
through Moses.

It is easy to think that this commandment
does not concern you because you don't
make physical idols that you bow down to
like the Israelites did, however, you may
have built idols in your heart that you don't
know about.

Anything you exalt above God is an idol. A
common idol in our modern world is
idolizing stuff. Many people have an
insatiable desire for more and more things
that they are willing to do anything to
acquire more stuff in their lives.

To bring it closer to home, since this book is about wealth, many people idolize money and put it above all else. Some would rather betray God and sin just so they can make money; they even have the audacity to say that it's okay because they can repent later and God will forgive them.

Idolatry cost the Israelites their promised land, and if you are not careful, it may cost you yours too. If you discover that you have built many idols in your heart, I would urge you to repent and submit yourself back to God. He must be our only God, we must serve him only.

5. Disobedience and Rebellion

Rebelling against God's word and his servants was another sin that cost the Israelites their promised land.

Today we see a lot of believers publicly insulting and speaking against servants of God. Social media has given us easy access to connect with different servants of God and a platform to spread the good news of salvation to the world. But instead of using it for good, many believers have now turned it into a weapon and an avenue to insult and attack their brothers and sisters in Christ.

Be very careful in how you speak to or
about servants of God. Even if you think
they are wrong, instead of attacking them
online have you considered taking them to
the Lord in prayer? Many believers forget
this simple principle about correction; it is
very difficult for one to receive correction
from someone they have no relationship
with. If you think that a person is wrong, and
you don't even know them personally, the
first thing to do is go to God in prayer. Pray
for the heart of your fellow believer that they
may find true repentance, pray that God will
send people to speak with the man in
question and that their hearts will be ready
to receive correction.

If that is not enough for you, you can meet
someone who has a relationship with the
person in question and share your concerns
with them and let them be the one to pass
on your concerns if they deem it fit.
Whatever you do, do not be part of those
keyboard warriors pouring out insults and
causing division in the body of Christ.

Even the Bible says that the world will know
we belong to Christ because of our love for
one another(John 13:35). Your lack of love

for a fellow believer is a telling sign that you are not a true disciple of Jesus.

Let's take Miriam and Aaron for example, in Numbers 12, they spoke against Moses because he was married to a foreign woman. By Jewish standards, Moses should not have married a foreigner. But since the hearts of Miriam and Aaron were rebellious, God punished them. They thought they were better than Moses and they gossiped and spoke about him behind his back. But God exposed them and His anger burned against them.

Numbers 12:1-2, 8-9 (NIV)
Miriam and Aaron began to talk against Moses because of his Cushite wife, for he had married a Cushite. "Has the Lord spoken only through Moses?" they asked. "Hasn't he also spoken through us?" And the Lord heard this.

With him I speak face to face, clearly and not in riddles; he sees the form of the Lord. Why then were you not afraid to speak against my servant Moses?"
The anger of the Lord burned against them, and he left them.

There are many more instances where God punished rebellion in the Israelites' camp; Korah led 250 men in a rebellion against Moses, and the ground opened up and swallowed them, their households, and all their belongings.

Today, we find that many people take God's word and his servants for granted, this is why their lives remain grounded.

If we want to experience genuine wealth, you and I must return to lead a lifestyle of holiness. We must commit to living with integrity and fear of the Lord.

Stop envying sinners because they seem to be wealthy. They are empty without God. Genuine wealth goes beyond money and fancy cars, it encompasses every area of your life including your mental, physical, spiritual, and emotional well-being. Genuine wealth comes without sorrow and it can only come from God. Genuine wealth is a byproduct of God's presence. Get back to the presence of God. Get back to Eden.

Chapter 2

Thinking

In the previous chapter, I mentioned that in order to change your life, you must change your mind. Who you are right now is the direct result of your thoughts and what you believe about yourself. Believe it or not, your moral compass, your reactions to situations, and even your core beliefs are shaped by your subconscious; things you have been taught and picked up throughout your lifetime.

Albert Einstein said you can't solve a problem using the same kind of thinking that created the problem in the first place. Our current way of thinking has brought us to our current state of life. If we want to have a better, wealthier life, our current mentality will not take us there. We need to change the way we think to match where we want to go.

Romans 12:2 (NLT)
Don't copy the behaviour and customs of this world, but let God transform you into a new person by changing the way you think. Then you will learn to know God's will for

you, which is good and pleasing and
perfect.

This is another key to genuine wealth. After praying, fasting, seeking the presence of God, and pursuing holiness, we must engage our minds if we want to be wealthy. It is the ability to think productively that can lead us to wealth. Many believers are crying out to God for money but God is waiting on them to engage their minds.

Thinking is what brings out brilliant business ideas. Thinking is what reminds you of the talent and gift you have and how you can use it to serve others and get paid for it. Thinking will remind you of what you have and teach you how you can apportion it to be a source of wealth for you.

Thinking is also what will convince you that you are capable of following through with that God-given idea. Your mentality and your way of thinking are what will give you the courage to pursue an investment even when you know there are risks involved. Thinking is what will help you solve problems at work and be considered an asset by your employer. Child of God, it is important that you engage your mind.

We Have the Mind of Christ

1 Corinthians 2:16 (NLT)

For, "Who can know the Lord's thoughts? Who knows enough to teach him?" But we understand these things, for we have the mind of Christ.

We have the mind of Christ and so we have understanding. And because we have the mind of Christ, our way of thinking must align with Christ's way of thinking.

By definition, thinking is the ability to coordinate your thoughts productively for increased output. It is your mind that instructs your body; your body just follows the instructions of your mentality. So for example, when you feel sick, your mind has told your body that you are sick. This is why sometimes someone can be completely healthy showing no symptoms, but the moment they get a diagnosis then all the symptoms start to display in their body. This is because their minds have accepted the sickness and the body starts acting accordingly. When they weren't diagnosed, their minds had not acknowledged any sickness and so the body remained unaware.

This is why the bible also says that we should guard our hearts because out of it flows the issues of life. Guarding our hearts is guarding our minds. Whatever enters your mind and into your subconscious is what you will believe about yourself and it is what will flow from your heart.

There are many sources of your thought process, it is up to you to identify where your thoughts come from and test them against scripture. Because you have the mind of Christ, you must eliminate any thoughts or ways of thinking that do not align with what God says about you.

Where Do Our Thoughts Come From?

Your environment
Thoughts can come from your environment, which means the people around you. They can come from your parents, your school, how you were raised, your friends, or your colleagues. Thoughts can also be influenced by the media; which encompasses news outlets, social media, movies, music, and any other material you consume.

This is why young adults can struggle with peer pressure. Their thoughts have been influenced by their peers and they have decided to take on the mentality of everyone else around them.

Since the media have constructed a "handsome" man to be tall, and dark you may find some women looking specifically for those qualities in a partner without really thinking about why they are doing so. Their thoughts have been so heavily influenced that it has become a part of their deal breakers.

The spirit realm
Your thoughts can also come from the spirit realm. Now, in the realm of the spirit you can either be influenced by the spirit of God or evil spirits. For example, when the devil tried to tempt Jesus when he was fasting, he didn't appear to Jesus physically. The temptations were through the mind. It was through his mind and imagination that he showed him the whole world and asked him to bow.

This is why we are asked to test every spirit. Everything that comes to your mind may not be from God. This is why you need to compare it with the word of God and see where it stands.

Usually, when thoughts come at us from either of the above sources, they then enter our conscious minds. If you mishandle the thoughts as they come through your conscious mind, they will then settle into your subconscious mind, which makes them part of your belief system. You can no longer control any thoughts in your subconscious mind which is why you need to handle them at the conscious level.

The subconscious mind can not be controlled. Psychologists say that 9 out of 10 things we do come out of our subconscious mind. That is why, when you are angry for example, you can find yourself saying something or doing something that shocks you because you didn't even know you had it in you. It is because of what has been deposited in your subconscious.

Even though you can't control what comes out of your subconscious, you can control what comes in. At the beginning of this chapter, we quoted Romans 12:2 which spoke about renewing your mind.

The only thing that can sanctify your subconscious and renew your mind is the word of God. When you start consuming the word of God consistently, your subconscious becomes filled with it with no room for any other thoughts. The word of God is likened to cleansing water that makes you holy and clean.

Ephesians 5:26 (NLT)
to make her holy and clean, washed by the cleansing of God's word.

Consume the word as often as you can, attend your local assembly and be edified in fellowship with other believers, listen to worship music, and consume content that will feed your spirit. Do not allow any evil thoughts to linger in your mind, capture and take authority over them using 2nd Corinthians 10:5.

2 Corinthians 10:5 (NLT)
We destroy every proud obstacle that keeps people from knowing God. We capture their rebellious thoughts and teach them to obey Christ.

Engage the Mind of Christ

Now we know that we have the mind of Christ. What does that look like in your daily life? It means that your mind and your thoughts must align with how Christ thinks.

The mind of Christ is the ability to think productively. If you engage the mind of Christ, then you will be able to produce things you thought were not possible. You will be able to see things the way Jesus sees them.

Where there are problems, you will see opportunities. You will not blame others for the challenges that you go through or for your life circumstances, because you know that all things work together for good for them that love God.

Because you have the mind of Christ, you will not hold on to jealousy, envy, or strife. How can God trust you with wealth if your heart is ridden with envy? You will not have time to focus on things that are beneficial to you if all you do is compare and try to compete with others out of jealousy.

Engaging the mind of Christ also means getting rid of all bitterness, malice, unforgiveness, backbiting, pettiness, and confusion. Did you know that things like bitterness and unforgiveness can actually make the physical body sick? You literally poison your own body by harbouring all these traits in your heart.

If you want to be wealthy, then you need to have a clear mind and a heart free from poison.

The ABC of Right Thinking

After recognizing the important role that thinking plays in our journey to wealth, we will now learn the right way of thinking.

1. Sit down

Yes! Take a seat and slow down. The problem is that we are always in a hurry, moving from one place to another. We hardly take the time to slow down and consider all the options.

Luke 14:28 (NLT)
For which of you, intending to build a tower, does not sit down first and count the cost, whether he has enough to finish it—

If you are always too busy and anxious, you miss out on the opportunity to truly count the cost and know all the facts before you begin a project. For you to produce the kind of wealth you desire, you need to learn to slow down, gather all the facts, and look at the results. You can ask yourself some questions and respond honestly. For example, you can ask yourself the following:

- Do you love what you do? What would you love to do even without getting paid?
- Is this the kind of output I desire? If not what do I need to change?
- Should I change the product?
- Should I change the location of the product?
- Is this product really needed or am I just following trends?
- Should I change my career or just find another job within my current career?

These questions will help you discover your zone of genius.

Depending on where you are in life, some of these questions can help you truly think about what you are doing. You can also come up with your own questions to help you pinpoint where you are.

The Bible tells us in Luke 14 that before you build a house, you need to first count the cost and see if you are able to finish it. Or before you go to war, you need to know your army's capabilities in comparison with the army you are going against. You don't just randomly wake up and start a project without considering the cost.

This happens to many of us in the body of Christ; God gives you an idea for business, work, or ministry, but instead of first submitting it back to him in prayer and sitting down to flesh it out, you rush out to tell everyone about it and even take first steps but you can't see it through to the end because you didn't take the time to count the cost.

Sitting down, especially sitting down with God, will help change your perspective and see things clearer. Sometimes the problems we face seem huge because we are seeing them from our own perspective and not Christ's perspective.

Ephesians 2:6 (NLT)
and raised us up together, and made us sit together in the heavenly places in Christ Jesus

Sitting down with God exchanges our myopic view of a situation with His perspective, which is the winning perspective. We are already seated with Christ in heavenly places, we are already above whatever circumstance we are experiencing now, we just have to engage our mind which is the mind of Christ.

So please, sit down with God to think through things. Always carry a paper and pen when you meet with God. Ask him questions and write down what he says. Write down strategies that will take you to your goal. Write down the thoughts that go through your mind, even if it seems like they are just your thoughts. Write everything down and later on, you can test it against the word of God to make sure it aligns.

Whatever you do, don't assume that you already know everything. Even what you think is the silliest thought can be the idea that revolutionizes your life. The greatest tragedy is for you to miss out on a good thing because you thought you could remember everything. Writing is a crucial part of the thinking process as we journey toward wealth.

Habakkuk 2:2 (NLT)

Then the Lord answered me and said:

"Write the vision

And make it plain on tablets,

That he may run who reads it.

2. Set time apart

Time is an essential commodity in bringing out the right results of wealth. For many of us, it is almost unimaginable to set time apart for thinking. If you are like me and grew up in an African household, you have probably heard the adults in your life ask you why you are thinking too much or point out that you are too young to be deep in thought.

However, if you want to excel you must take some time to think and reflect on your life. Thinking helps you come up with fresh ideas, discover yourself more, answer deep questions of your heart, or even hear God more clearly.

In today's world, we are constantly distracted by noise. From the moment you wake up, you reach out for your cell phone and spend time checking emails, checking the news, or scrolling on social media. On your daily commute, you are probably listening to more news, a book or a podcast, or even just music. There is no time when you aren't consuming some form of content, your mind fails to get a break.

Setting time to think allows you to go deep and even get inspired thoughts from the Holy Spirit. Let's take Daniel for example, in Daniel 2 he was summoned by King Nebuchadnezzar to interpret a dream for him. Daniel asked the king to give him time. He took some time to discuss with his friends and also time to ask the Lord and hear from him. And God answered him in a dream. If he had not taken some time to ask God, he might not have received an answer.

Daniel 2:16 (NLT)
So Daniel went in and asked the king to give him time, that he might tell the king the interpretation.

Sometimes, when we face a problem we immediately run to Google or social media or our peers to find the solution. Instead, let us run to God and set some time to think. In our silence and in the absence of external noise, the Holy Spirit will show us the solutions we so desperately seek elsewhere.

3. Research

After setting time apart to think and hear from God, you need to research. You need to be informed if you want to be transformed. As the saying goes, to be uninformed is to be deformed.

We see many examples of research from the Bible; Daniel understood by the books that Israel's captivity has gone on longer than it should, and he used that understanding to pray strategically and inquire of the Lord. Paul, even in his dying moments requested for his books to be brought to him. He understood the value of studying, and that is why he taught Timothy to study to show himself approved.

Seek to understand by researching. Read books, listen to those who have gone ahead of you, and use the internet as a resource for your learning and growth.

Some assignments even require you to go back to school. Knowledge and understanding is very important in your quest for wealth. You can't reject knowledge and still expect wealth.

To think well, you need to have all the facts.
And you can get the facts through research.
Decisions made on quality information will
lead to a distinction. Do not just take
everything at face value, seek out relevant
materials in the areas you are looking to
succeed in.

Study the people in your field and buy their
products. See what they are doing right or
wrong. Ask them questions. And whatever
you do, do not attack them because you can
never attract what you attack.

Instead of seeing those who have gone
ahead of you as competition, celebrate
them and learn from them. You do not have
to do what you do the way they did it, you
can always add your own uniqueness and
improve on what they did, however,
recognize that they paved the way for you.

   4.   Meditation

By definition, meditation is a process where we acquire relevant information for quality decisions. In Hebrew, it is *hagah* while in Greek it is *meletaou,* which means to think, to think deeply, to muse or to reflect. It also means to mutter or whisper to yourself, to ponder, or to make a quiet sound such as sighing.

The Hebrew meaning is an active recitation. For example, meditating on scriptures is to quietly repeat them in soft droning sounds while utterly abandoning outside distractions. Meditation is tuning into the frequency of the spiritual world to the point where you capture spiritual thoughts.

For the sake of this book, we will use thinking and meditation interchangeably.

Most people say that they do not know how to meditate, but the same people know how to worry. If you worry, you can definitely meditate. Worrying is paying attention, overthinking, and pondering over a negative outcome of a certain circumstance.

Instead of spending your time worrying or meditating on the negative, you can dedicate your time to meditating on the positive and the things you want to achieve.

When you meditate, your feelings, behaviour, and even your body move in the direction of your meditation. That is why you may be speaking to someone who says they are happy for you but their body language says otherwise. This means in their heart, they are not truly happy for you so no matter what they say with their mouth, their bodies betray them because their bodies follow the direction of their meditation.

Meditation Changes the Way You Behave

As I mentioned earlier, to change your life, you must change the way you think. Many of us try to change our habits before we change our way of thinking, forgetting that the habits we have now are a direct result of our thinking.

This is why many people struggle to accomplish their new year's resolutions. In fact, most people drop their resolutions before the first quarter of the year. Think about it, how often have you had the same resolution each year and still failed to accomplish it?

This happens because you maintained the same way of thinking and tried to accomplish a different result. Unfortunately, it does not work that way. To accomplish different results you must update your thought process, which in turn changes your habits.

Are you Carnally Minded or Spiritually Minded?

In changing your mind, you can either be carnally minded or spiritually minded. In Romans 8, the bible tells us that there are two forces that control our minds, the spirit and the flesh. The Spirit leads us to life and peace while the flesh leads us to sin and death.

Romans 8:6 (NLT)
So letting your sinful nature control your mind leads to death. But letting the Spirit control your mind leads to life and peace.

It is obvious that to yield a successful and peaceful life, your thoughts should be powered by the Holy Spirit. But you may ask, how do you get the Spirit of God to control your mind?

The answer is simple: meditate on the word of God. The word of God is spirit and it is life, it empowers you and gives you direction, instructions, and strategies. There is nothing you are looking for that you can't receive from the word. Saving and investing strategies are in the word of God, creativity, and art is found there.

Above all, because you have a relationship with God, He will give you ideas for wealth and the blueprint on how to go about executing it. He will instruct you on who to partner with, books to read, resources to pay attention to, and just general step-by-step directions on what to do. The only thing you need to do is be sure to obey everything He instructs you to do.

Joshua 1:8 (NLT)
Study this Book of Instruction continually. Meditate on it day and night so you will be sure to obey everything written in it. Only then will you prosper and succeed in all you do.

Psalms 1:2-3 (NLT)
But they delight in the law of the LORD, meditating on it day and night. They are like

trees planted along the riverbank, bearing fruit each season. Their leaves never wither, and they prosper in all they do.

Success is What You Think

The mind is a battlefield and a fertile ground. It is a battlefield because you have to war for your thoughts to align with what you want for your life. It is also a fertile ground because whatever you plant in it grows and bears fruit.

It is up to you to decide what you want to plant in your mind and the kind of fruit you want to bear. What grows in your mind right now determines the fruit you want to bear later.

Anything you set your mind to achieve is possible. Every product you use was once a thought that someone had. Every achievement started with a thought. What do you see in your mind's eye? What dreams do you have for yourself? Are your thoughts aligned to match what you want to achieve?

When your mind is right, even problems become opportunities. For example, in

Winnipeg, Manitoba where I live, the winters are so brutal. When it snows, so many of us complain about the cold and the piles of snow that gather on the roads. However, there are some people who make a living from this situation that we complain about. There are people who are excited about the snow because they have built thriving businesses, clearing snow and helping others to do so. Instead of a problem, they saw an opportunity. That is the power of right thinking on display.

You must reprogram your mind and align your thoughts with what God says. Your quality of life can never be better than the quality of your thoughts.

Your mind is the breeding ground for ideas and creativity. Your creativity is what will enable you to chart a new path or course of action.

God did not use cash to create the world, he saw it in his mind, spoke into existence, and even got down in the mud to form man and breathe life into him. But it all started in his mind. Similarly, God did not create the chair or the cellphone, he gave men the ideas and they used their minds and experiences to create these items we now enjoy.

Your thoughts inspire your actions, which inspire the outcome of your life.

Change the Way You Think

So now you may be asking yourself, how do you change the way you think? This is what you can do to ensure your meditations are aligned with God's.

Your mind is like a soccer ball, it can bounce from one place to another. The way to combat that is to make sure it is directed by God's word. The only way to change your mind is to tie it to the word of God.

This does not necessarily mean positive thinking; positive thinking is different from scriptural thinking. Scripture is what has the power to renew your mind as we learned earlier from Romans 12.

Romans 12:2 (NLT)
Don't copy the behaviour and customs of this world, but let God transform you into a new person by changing the way you think. Then you will learn to know God's will for you, which is good and pleasing and perfect.

Part of changing the way you think is also acknowledging that you do not know everything. No matter how smart you are, you can't trust your thoughts to be aligned with God's thoughts. Renewing your mind requires a certain level of intentionality. Because God's thoughts are not like ours, we must be intentional about renewing our minds with His word if we want to change the way we think.

Isaiah 55:8-9 (NLT)
*"My thoughts are nothing like your thoughts," says the LORD.
"And my ways are far beyond anything you could imagine.
For just as the heavens are higher than the earth,
so my ways are higher than your ways and my thoughts higher than your thoughts.*

You must be intentional about getting rid of all the weeds that cause you to have a negative mindset. Weeds like anger, fear, and just negative environments are a hindrance to your way of thinking.

Anger hinders us from thinking like God. This is why the bible says that we can be angry but not sin, which means that anger can lead us to sin, which takes us out of God's presence, and in turn out of wealth.

Ecclesiastes 7:9 (NLT)
Control your temper, for anger labels you a fool.

Fear robs us of our hope, vitality, and life. What you fear is actually what you attract and it is what you become. By fear, I don't only mean physical fear but also emotional fear. You find that even when God gives us that million-dollar idea, we are still stuck in poverty because we are too afraid to pursue it. But God encourages us to overcome fear because He is with us at all times. We have no reason to be afraid.

Isaiah 41:10 (NLT)
Don't be afraid, for I am with you.
Don't be discouraged, for I am your God.
I will strengthen you and help you.
I will hold you up with my victorious right hand.

If you want to change the way you think, you must ensure a conducive environment for your mind to thrive. Get rid of all negativity from your environment. All thoughts that don't align with your faith should be uprooted. Surround yourself with people who speak life. Do not indulge in gossip and mindless conversations. Get rid of hatred, insecurities, envy, and even guilt.

Mastering your thoughts means you are well on your way to genuine wealth.

Chapter 3

Conversing your way to Wealth

I can almost hear your thoughts saying, "It can't possibly be that easy. There is no way you can talk your way to wealth. If it was that easy, everyone would be doing it". I had the same thought when I learned about this.

Before we get into it, let us first define the conversation. A conversation, according to Merriam-Webster's dictionary, is an oral exchange of sentiments, observations, opinions, or ideas. Since it is an oral exchange, it must be vocal or spoken out loud so that your message can be heard by the recipient.

No doubt you have had many conversations in the course of your life but the conversation we will be focusing on on our journey to wealth is the conversation you have with yourself.

We have already established that what you believe about yourself carries so much weight if you want to be wealthy. While a lot of things could have been said about you throughout your life, it is not the water outside that sinks a ship but the water that gets into the ship. What people say about you does not carry as much impact as what you say about yourself.

What you believe about yourself is what you become. The belief about yourself comes from hearing what you say to yourself. Therefore, what you say about yourself is what you believe about yourself which will eventually be who you become.

Are You Kind to Yourself?

Have you noticed how quick and easy it is for you to encourage a friend who is going through a hard time or doesn't believe in themselves? You know all the right things to say and all the scripture to encourage them but when it comes to you, you don't extend yourself the same grace.

Be careful what you say to and about yourself. What you hear is what you believe and what you believe is eventually what you become. Speak kindly to yourself and remember to encourage yourself.

1 Samuel 30:6
And David was greatly distressed; for the people spake of stoning him, because the soul of all the people was grieved, every man for his sons and for his daughters: but David encouraged himself in the LORD his God.

When David was going through one of the darkest times of his life, he encouraged himself in the Lord. He spoke tenderly to himself. It doesn't matter what is currently going on in your world, the words you speak to yourself will determine if you will survive and move on or remain stuck in your current mindset.

The more you speak kindly to yourself and declare God's word over yourself, the more you start to believe it and eventually become the very thing you were saying. Conversely, the more you speak ill of yourself, the more you believe it and eventually become what you believe.

Proverbs 18:21 (NLT)
The tongue can bring death or life; those who love to talk will reap the consequences.

Speak It Out

Our words have creative power, what we say is what we see in our world. You can not become a wealthy person if your conversations don't align with your desires.

When God created the heavens and earth in Genesis 1, He did not hold back from speaking what he wanted to see. The Bible tells us that whatever he said happened. When he said "Let there be light", then there was. Everything he said, he saw.

We are like Him because He created us in His image and likeness. We have to use our words to shape our world.

Psalms 107:2 (NLT)
Has the LORD redeemed you? Then speak out!
Tell others he has redeemed you from your enemies.

What makes what you say about yourself more powerful is saying it out loud. Be vocal about your identity and what God has said about you. Speak words of life over yourself so you can hear them. The Bible says that faith comes by hearing, so even if you don't believe what you're saying about yourself yet, after hearing it consistently over a period of time, you will start to believe it and eventually become exactly who you say you are.

What you become is a result of what you tell yourself, so you can choose to degrade yourself or empower and encourage yourself. The word

Chapter 4

The Love Connection

The journey to wealth goes beyond your finances, it usually envelopes every aspect of your life. If other aspects of your life are lacking, it is quite challenging to attain the genuine wealth you are looking for.

God wants us to have an abundant life, and an abundant life is not just financial well-being, it includes your health, your relationships, and even your peace of mind.

John 10:10 (AMP)
The thief comes only in order to steal and kill and destroy. I came that they may have and enjoy life, and have it in abundance [to the full, till it overflows].

Another translation of this verse says "I have come so that you may have a rich and satisfying life". When you think about it, a rich and satisfying life is a life void of sickness, broken relationships, or even mental health challenges. A rich and satisfying life is a well-rounded and fulfilling life. This is the genuine wealth we desire.

Love plays a huge part in having an abundant life. We can not be victorious in life if we do not walk in love. God is love, therefore, walking out of love is walking away from God. We already know that genuine wealth can only come from God's presence, so a lack of love is a lack of wealth.

A wealthy person is someone who has mastered love. For you to display wealth there are 5 key areas you need to display love:

Love for God

Mark 12:29-30 (NLT)
Jesus replied, "The most important commandment is this: 'Listen, O Israel! The LORD our God is the one and only LORD. 30 And you must love the LORD your God with all your heart, all your soul, all your mind, and all your strength.'

Loving God is not just a nice thing to do, it is a commandment. In fact, Jesus says that it is the most important commandment of all and the entire law and requirements of the prophets are based on this command (Matthew 22:40).

The Greek word for love is *agapao*, which

means to love unconditionally and sacrificially as God himself does. This kind of love is not an emotion, it is an action that is initiated by choice.

The kind of love for God we are speaking about here is not dependent on what God does or does not do for you. It goes deeper than what He gives you; it is unconditional love. When love is viewed only as a feeling, it is diminished in its true meaning. Loving someone because of what they give you, or because they are kind to you simply means that if they ever change, you will no longer feel the same way. Your love was simply a feeling based on your current circumstances.

But that is not the way we are commanded to love. We are commanded to love God with all our heart, soul, and strength. What does that look like?

Loving God with your heart means loving him with your emotions. Yes, you should love God with your emotions but that should not be the only way you love God. Your heart is the center of your being, which includes your emotions and even your will. Willfully choose to love God, make him a priority and the center of your life.

To love God with all your soul means to love him with your mind, your reasoning, and your understanding. It means to love God with your intellect. Our mind must be submitted to Him. This is why we renew our minds daily with the word of God so that we can be fully submitted to Him even in our thoughts.

And finally, love the Lord your God with all your strength. This is the physical part of you. It means actively loving God with your actions. Our physical bodies will follow what our hearts and minds are tuned to. If our inner desire is to love God, then our actions (which are powered by our physical bodies) will show it.

John 14:15 (AMP)
"If you [really] love Me, you will keep and obey My commandments.

The true measure of our love for God is our obedience to Him. If you love him, you will obey his commands. Your heart will incline to what He is saying, your mind will accept it and your actions will prove your love for him. Every true lover of God is an obedient child of God.

Love for Your Spouse

There is a connection between genuine wealth and having a stable and happy spouse. A study done by Washington University in St. Louis found that a happy home or a great spouse plays a big role in an individual's career advancement. It said that having a conscientious spouse improves your performance at work thus making you excel in your career.

A career is only one aspect of what loving your spouse can achieve. A happy marriage means happy and healthy individuals who can perform their duties with support from their partners. They are not distracted by petty arguments or lack of peace in their home which allows them to perform better in every other aspect of their life.

The Bible also tells us about the benefits and consequences of loving our spouses. When you can genuinely love your wife you will be blessed. The blessing is beyond riches, God's blessing includes health, wealth, safety, joy, fulfillment, and an all-around abundant life.

Malachi 2:14 (NLT)

You cry out, "Why doesn't the LORD accept my worship?" I'll tell you why! Because the LORD witnessed the vows you and your wife

made when you were young. But you have
been unfaithful to her, though she remained
your faithful partner, the wife of your
marriage vows.

Wives are encouraged to honor their
husbands and husbands are encouraged to
love their wives. Naturally, women are
lovers, this is why Scripture reminds them
to honour and submit to their husbands.
They do not need a reminder to love
because that comes naturally to them.
Husbands, on the other hand, are reminded
to love because that doesn't come naturally
to them. Scripture even goes further to tell
husbands that their prayers may be
hindered if they don't treat their wives well.

1 Peter 3:7 (NLT)
In the same way, you husbands must give
honour to your wives. Treat your wife with
understanding as you live together. She
may be weaker than you are, but she is
your equal partner in God's gift of new life.
Treat her as you should so your prayers will
not be hindered.

Ephesians 5:21-23 (NLT)
And further, submit to one another out of
reverence for Christ. For wives, this means
submit to your husbands as to the Lord. For

a husband is the head of his wife as Christ is the head of the church. He is the Savior of his body, the church

Ephesians 5:25-26, 28 (NLT)
For husbands, this means love your wives, just as Christ loved the church. He gave up his life for her to make her holy and clean, washed by the cleansing of God's word. He did this to present her to himself as a glorious church without a spot or wrinkle or any other blemish. Instead, she will be holy and without fault. In the same way, husbands ought to love their wives as they love their own bodies. For a man who loves his wife actually shows love for himself.

Love for Your Family

Your family includes not only your blood family members but also your brothers and sisters in Christ.

If you want genuine wealth, you must love your family. Loving your family means looking out for each other, helping each other out, giving support, and bearing one another's burdens among many other things.

1 John 4:20-21 (NLT)
If someone says, "I love God," but hates

a fellow believer,[c] that person is a liar;
for if we don't love people we can see,
how can we love God, whom we cannot
see? And he has given us this command:
Those who love God must also love their
fellow believers.

If you love God then show love to your
brothers. We want to see your love for
God by how you love your family.

Love for Others

When you think of loving others, you can't
help but think of the parable of the Good
Samaritan. In this parable, a man was
attacked by robbers and left half dead.
Many people, including religious leaders,
passed by the man on the street but refused
to help him. Until a Samaritan passed by
and took pity on him and helped him out.
One of the greatest lessons in this parable
is that love is not only reserved for the
people you know or have a relationship
with. Loving others requires you to show
compassion and help to strangers. The
Bible calls it the second greatest
commandment.

Matthew 22:37-40 (NLT)
Jesus replied, "'You must love the LORD
your God with all your heart, all your soul,
and all your mind.' This is the first and

greatest commandment. A second is equally important: 'Love your neighbour as yourself.' The entire law and all the demands of the prophets are based on these two commandments."

Love for Yourself

Many find it easier to love God and others but not themselves. But scripture tells us that we can not really love others if we don't love ourselves. You can't give what you don't have, so if you don't love yourself you can't love others.

Learn to love yourself, appreciate where you are and celebrate the grace of God upon your life. You can't attract wealth if you consistently despise and look down on yourself.

God does not make mistakes. When He created you, He made you in his image and likeness. This means that when you look at yourself in the mirror, you see God because you look like him.

God loves you not because of what you have done but because He just loves you. He still loves you even if you don't pray, fast, or don't give tithe. It's not because of what you do but it is who He is.

1 John 4:8 (NLT)

*But anyone who does not love does not
know God, for God is love.*

When you learn to love, you will attract
wealth. Unfortunately, many people think
that love is just a feeling. We have been
sold the lie that love starts and stops at
feelings. While feelings are involved when
you love, love is so much more than
feelings.

Love is a commitment; a promise that
regardless of what comes you are
committed to love. Paul's first letter to the
Corinthians described love perfectly. When
you read through it you discover that some
attributes of love are attributes of a wealthy
person.

1 Corinthians 13:4-7 (AMP)
*Love endures with patience and serenity,
love is kind and thoughtful, and is not
jealous or envious; love does not brag and
is not proud or arrogant. It is not rude; it is
not self-seeking, it is not provoked [nor
overly sensitive and easily angered]; it does
not take into account a wrong endured. It
does not rejoice at injustice, but rejoices
with the truth [when right and truth prevail].
Love bears all things [regardless of what*

comes], believes all things [looking for the best in each one], hopes all things [remaining steadfast during difficult times], endures all things [without weakening].

Love is what will keep you going when everything is difficult or seems to be falling apart. Love brings perseverance. Love is what will make people like you; it will build your reputation. You may think that it doesn't matter if people like you but people do business with people they know, like and trust. How will they know, like and trust you? They will know because of how you love.

If you desire genuine wealth, your life must be characterized by love.

Chapter 5

Order Your Life

One of the keys to living a successful life is having order in your life. Nothing thrives in chaos. In the business world, companies that do well are those that have order and a structure in place to support growth.

Even investors don't invest in chaotic organizations. In fact, one of the basic things that a good investor learns is to research the organization they want to invest in. In this research, they learn to study the organization's structure, its financials and even its plans for future growth. These studies are what determine whether they will invest their money or not.

If this is what it is like in the business world, then it is definitely no different for anyone who desires genuine wealth. Order is the basic foundation for having structure and building systems which eventually foster growth and lead to success.

The advantages of having order in your life are not only limited to the business world, you need to have order in every aspect of your life. Even in your prayer life, receiving from God requires a certain level of order and stillness. We will discuss this more when we talk about spiritual order.

If your life is not in order, no one can commit true riches into your hands. Even miracles require a certain level of order. For example, in John 6:9-13, Jesus performs the miracle of feeding thousands with only two fish and five loaves of bread. But before he could do that, he first asked the disciples to let everyone sit down orderly. Nothing thrives in chaos. Miracles require a certain level of order and organization.

Create an Atmosphere for the Flow

For you to attract wealth, you need to create an atmosphere for wealth to flow to you. Nothing thrives in a chaotic environment. Just think about it, when your life is chaotic that is when you get anxious. When things around you are chaotic, people avoid you. A chaotic life can even affect your health. All these things and more are detrimental to your overall success.

When there is chaos in your home, in your marriage, or in your church, it affects your overall well-being. When you panic, you affect the flow of resources to you. Lack of order affects the flow of your life.

Order does not only mean a properly arranged space or a meticulously organized life. Order starts from within. There has to be order in your mind, order in your spirit and even order in your body. You need to be grounded and centred, you need to be grounded and not easily moved.

Psalms 92:12-14 (NKJV)
The righteous shall flourish like a palm tree,
He shall grow like a cedar in Lebanon.
Those who are planted in the house of the
LORD
Shall flourish in the courts of our God.
They shall still bear fruit in old age;
They shall be fresh and flourishing,

The Bible says those that are planted are the ones that will flourish because when you are planted it shows stability. The scriptures often use trees to symbolize believers and how their life should be. Lebanon cedars are big, magnificent trees

that can grow to a whopping 40 metres.
They are immovable, stable and represent
luxury and wealth.

In fact, in Ezekiel 31, God compared
Assyria's greatness to the Lebanon cedars;

Indeed Assyria was a cedar in Lebanon,
With fine branches that shaded the forest,
And of high stature;
And its top was among the thick boughs.

The waters made it grow;
Underground waters gave it height,
With their rivers running around the place
where it was planted,
And sent out rivulets to all the trees of the
field.

'Therefore its height was exalted above
all the trees of the field;
Its boughs were multiplied,
And its branches became long because of
the abundance of water,
As it sent them out.

All the birds of the heavens made their
nests in its boughs;
Under its branches all the beasts of the
field brought forth their young;
And in its shadow all great nations made
their home.

This is what God desires for you and me. To be planted, stable and flourishing like a cedar. That we will grow branches that other people can nest in and bear fruit to benefit everyone around us. Our wealth and success are not just about us, God gives us wealth to also benefit everyone around us for his glory. But none of this is possible without order.

Create an atmosphere that allows the flow of wealth to you. As much as it is in your power, get rid of anything that will cause chaos in your life. Do you need schedules to stay organized? Start creating and following a schedule. Do you need to delegate more? Do so as soon as you can. Do whatever you need to do to have order in your life.

Spiritual Order

All aspects of your life require order, even your spiritual life requires order. What is spiritual order? The main premise of spiritual order is obedience. Whatever God tells you to do, you should do it.
Spiritual order is the most important order in your life. It sets the stage for every other aspect of your life because nothing happens in the physical before it happens in the spirit.

Deuteronomy 28:1-2 (NKJV)

Now it shall come to pass, if you diligently obey the voice of the LORD your God, to observe carefully all His commandments which I command you today, that the LORD your God will set you high above all nations of the earth. And all these blessings shall come upon you and overtake you, because you obey the voice of the LORD your God

You can't pick and choose the spiritual laws you want to follow. If you want to live in the blessings of obedience listed in the rest of Deuteronomy 28, you must be sure to obey everything and not only those things that are convenient for you.

This is the result of spiritual order. When you diligently obey the voice of God, everything else falls into place. That doesn't mean that you won't face challenges, but it means that even in the challenges, God is with you and there is a purpose to every pain.

He will make everything work together for your good because you love him and you live according to his commands.

Roman 8:28 (NLT)

And we know that God causes everything to work together for the good of those who love God and are called according to his purpose for them.

Emotional Order

Your emotions are a huge part of who you are and how you live your life. A lot of believers are of the opinion that emotions are unimportant because they are from the flesh.

I beg to differ.

Yes, your emotions can definitely influence your decisions and your way of life to the extent that you live in the flesh and disobey the Spirit of God in you. However, emotions are God-given gifts that signal the state of your heart. They aren't evil and they should not be ignored.

God created us in His image and likeness, which means that we are like Him. He has emotions just as much as we do. This is why in scripture we read about God feeling angry, jealous, and proud of His children. He experienced a range of emotions.

The only thing we need to understand is that we should not let our emotions lead us to sin. In as much as your emotions are valid, they can not be an excuse to sin.

Your mind is where your emotions are. Since we have learned the importance of a renewed mind in the pursuit of wealth and success, then we can't ignore our emotions. Emotions are important to the stability of the mind.

This is why you should also be mindful of emotional order. Peace of mind is underrated in how significant it is in the pursuit of wealth. Many of us have a lot of baggage to deal with that can cause us to be unstable in our emotions.

Even mental conditions like depression can sometimes come because the mind is being attacked which affects our emotions and goes on to affect the rest of the flow of our lives. Do you notice how one event that affects your mood negatively has the ability to affect the rest of your day, including your productivity and even your relationship with your loved ones?

This is why you can not trivialize your emotional health. Emotional order should be a priority in your life.

James 1:6-8 (NIV)

But when you ask, you must believe and not doubt, because the one who doubts is like a wave of the sea, blown and tossed by the wind. That person should not expect to receive anything from the Lord. Such a person is double-minded and unstable in all they do.

The scriptures say that a double-minded person who is unstable in what they do, which means a person lacking emotional order, should not expect to receive anything from the Lord!

Take heed and be mindful of your emotions. Seek help through prayer, wise counsel and medical help where necessary. In this age where a lot of believers villainize therapy, be part of the wise believers who takes advantage of tools like therapy and even encourage others to do the same.

Family Order

The home is the most important unit in society. If there are no thriving homes then there are no thriving individuals in the society. Any change you desire to see in the world starts from having healthy homes and healthy families.

Once there is no peace in the home there can never be a flow of resources. A chaotic family life is not a conducive atmosphere for the flow of wealth.

Genesis 18:19 (NLT)
I have singled him out so that he will direct his sons and their families to keep the way of the LORD by doing what is right and just. Then I will do for Abraham all that I have promised."

Look at Abraham, for example, God singled him out to bless him because he knew that Abraham wil lead his family well and teach them the ways of the Lord. There is a blessing that follows those whose families are taught and follow the way of the Lord.

There are many adults who are struggling now because of trauma from their families. They experienced some disturbing circumstances in their childhood and they still live in the effects of it as adults.

Apart from childhood trauma and the family
you grew up in, the family you start can
also have the same effect on you. If there
is no peace in your home and no unity with
your spouse, then there is no family order.
And we already know that the lack of order
is a recipe for failure.

Proverbs 19:13 (NIV)
A foolish child is a father's ruin,
and a quarrelsome wife is like
the constant dripping of a leaky roof.

We can't choose the family we come from
but we can definitely choose the family we
start. If you come from a dysfunctional
family, make sure a dysfunctional family
doesn't come from you.

Physical and Health Order

It is unfortunate that most believers think
that taking care of your physical health is
vanity or signifies a lack of faith. That could
not be any further from the truth. Our
bodies are the vessels that we use for our
lives here on Earth.

How can you pray for a successful and
prosperous life but not live long enough to

enjoy it because of health issues? Some issues can be avoided simply by taking care of our health. This is also God's desire for us.

3 John 1:2 (NLT)

Dear friend, I hope all is well with you and that you are as healthy in body as you are strong in spirit.

1 Corinthians 6:20 (AMP)

You were bought with a price [you were actually purchased with the precious blood of Jesus and made His own]. So then, honour and glorify God with your body.

Your body is also the temple that houses the Holy Spirit. What does your temple look like? Have you adorned it with proper covering? Have you filled your temple with so much junk and refused to take care of it? Have you used your temple to house other idols? Have you invited strange and foreign spirits into your temple? Have you allowed strange men and women to do what they please with your temple?

When you look through scripture you see how the temple of God was held in high regard. The temple was built with the best material, adorned with the finest linen and even furnished and filled with precious metals. The temple of God was honoured and revered by all.

In the New Testament, we see Jesus get very upset because the people mistreated the temple of God and used it for their personal business instead of for God's purpose. In Matthew 21, Jesus gets so angry that he flips tables at the temple and chases away all who are abusing the temple's purpose.

Do you take the same approach with your body? We are so used to living as we please and forgetting that our bodies are temples and they are important. Making time to exercise and eat healthy, spending time to dress well and being presentable are not vanity metrics. They are important and play a vital role in your life.

Beyond looking and feeling good, taking care of your body means taking care of your health. Some diseases are a result of poor lifestyle choices. Some sicknesses can be overturned just by changing your lifestyle and being more mindful of your health.

God wants you to fulfill your purpose, He wants you to accomplish His will for your life but you can not do that if your health is not in order. You can not operate at your maximum capacity if you're struggling with health issues.

If you want to live a successful life, do not leave your health to chance.

Chapter 6

The Mystery of Faith

The basis of the life of a believer is faith. You have probably heard it over and over again, "Have faith", "If you believe it, you can achieve it" or even "Faith it till you make it". Rightly so! Faith is what brings us through many situations. Faith is a powerful mystery.

Faith is what makes us Christians. To receive the gift of salvation all we had to do is confess with our mouths and believe in our hearts that Jesus came, died and rose again for our sins. It sounds so simple yet its impact is life-altering. This is why it is a mystery.

Everything you desire, you can achieve as long as you have faith. Wealth is no different, you need faith to be who you were called to be and to achieve the success you so desire.

Hebrews 11:1 (NKJV)
Now faith is the substance of things hoped for, the evidence of things not seen.

Faith reveals to us that there is another reality, even though we don't currently see it. There is a reality we are hoping for and believing in. And even though we don't see it, we know that it is more real than our current reality and we know that it is only a matter of time before it comes to pass.

Hebrews 11:6 (NKJV)
But without faith it is impossible to please Him, for he who comes to God must believe that He is, and that He is a rewarder of those who diligently seek Him.

God rewards those who have faith, He is pleased by them. In Hebrews 11, scripture tells us of the many great men and women whose great faith led to great rewards. From Abraham to Moses to the prophets, their faith is what made the difference.

You Have ALL You Need

Everything that we need for life has already been given to us. Just like in the Garden of Eden, God had made provision for man before he created man. He had a place to live, work to do, food to eat, and every other need you can think of. God had already anticipated man's needs and desires and provided for them.

Similarly, God is still in the business of providing for His people. He has already prepared everything you need to live a successful and fulfilling life. Everything has already been made available for you, you only need to access it.

2 Peter 1:3 (NKJV)

...as His divine power has given to us all things that pertain to life and godliness, through the knowledge of Him who called us by glory and virtue

Accessing what God has prepared is where a lot of us struggle. We get disappointed when things don't go the way we want them to. We get discouraged and then end up giving up on God.

If you want to succeed, giving up is not an option. As long as you know what God has said about your life, then it is only a matter of time, it will come to pass if you're willing to trust Him.

You may be wondering why it feels like sometimes your faith does not produce the results you desire. There are a few reasons that could be affecting your faith that we will discuss. The number one limiter of our faith is fear.

Why Are You Afraid?

Romans 10:17 (NKJV)
So then faith comes by hearing, and hearing by the word of God.

Just like how faith comes from hearing the word of God, fear also comes from hearing, but in this case, it is hearing what is against the word of God. Fear comes from hearing and meditating on lies. Fear's demand is to compromise the truth of God's word.

What and who you listen to makes all the difference. You can't trust God and nurture fear at the same time, one must give way. What you hear becomes what you meditate on and eventually becomes what you believe. And you already know that your belief will shape your life decisions.

Mark 4:24 (AMP)
Then He said to them, "Pay attention to what you hear. By your own standard of measurement [that is, to the extent that you study spiritual truth and apply godly wisdom] it will be measured to you [and

89

you will be given even greater ability to
respond]—and more will be given to you
besides.

The only way to get rid of fear and build up
your faith is by the study of scripture.
Scripture is the truth, the breathed-upon
word of God that is alive and has the power
to transform. Be diligent in the study of the
word. The more you know the truth, the
more you replace every lie you believe.

In studying the word you will find out what
God says about you, you will receive
wisdom and power to make wealth. You will
know your rights and even know how to
direct your prayer.

Let's take Daniel as an example, he
studied scripture and found out that
Jerusalem will be desolate for only 70
years (Daniel 9). But by that time they had
already gone past 70 years of bondage.
Armed with that knowledge and word of
truth, he went to God in prayer and
received a response right away. He was
able to pray with understanding and armed
with truth.

That is how you build your faith and
overcome fear. You can hold God to his

word and he will answer you. Because you know what he says, fear will no longer be a hindrance to your growth.

Fear, Be Gone!

So how do you deal with fear? Here are a few ways you can "faith it till you make it" and refuse to believe the lies of the enemy.

- Understand that fear is not your inheritance: God has not given you a spirit of fear but of power, love and a sound mind. Refuse to be trapped in the enemy's web of lies that cause you to be afraid. Fear is not of God.

Romans 8:15 (NLT)
So you have not received a spirit that makes you fearful slaves. Instead, you received God's Spirit when he adopted you as his own children.[h] Now we call him, "Abba, Father."

- Refuse to accept fearful thoughts: you don't use your thoughts to cancel out negative thoughts, you use your words. Declare your faith out loud and speak the truth to counter the lie that causes you to fear. You have the power to rebuke any lie that comes your way and replace it with the truth of God's word. Submit all your fears and cares to God in prayer and surrender them there.

2 Corinthians 10:5 (NKJV)

casting down arguments and every high thing that exalts itself against the knowledge of God, bringing every thought into captivity to the obedience of Christ

- Receive and believe the love of God: Understand your redemption rights as a child of God. When you understand the full measure of what Christ did for you and me on the cross of Calvary, you will receive his overwhelming love and accept that you are safe and secure in him.

2 Timothy 1:7 (NKJV)

For God has not given us a spirit of fear, but of power and of love and of a sound mind.

- Surround yourself with faith-filled people: who you have around you matters in determining what you believe. Some people inspire your confidence in God and help you to trust him more while others drain you of any faith you may have. The company you keep is a reflection of who you are and who you want to be.

Proverbs 27:17 (NLT)
As iron sharpens iron,
so a friend sharpens a friend.

Why are You Offended?

Offence is another aspect that can really affect your faith. When you're offended you start looking for reasons to avoid God; you slowly become absent from your prayer time, you refuse to speak to others, you start avoiding church gatherings and you slowly isolate yourself.

Offence can be silent but very deadly. Before you know it, offence can eat you up inside and cause you to stop believing in anything good. The sad part is that we usually justify the feeling and so if not careful, it may take a long time to recognize the negative effect it has caused on you.

Do yourself a favour and release offence. It is not worth the pain it's causing you. This doesn't mean that people won't offend you, unfortunately, that can't be avoided. Offences will come but it is how you deal with them that matters. Don't hold on to any pain that will cost you the full and successful life God has intended for you.

Why are You Bitter?

Bitterness happens when an offence has taken root in your heart and has grown. Bitterness is so poisonous and can hinder any forward movement toward a successful life.

If you want to bear good fruit, you must be mindful of the soil where you plant your seeds. It is the quality of the soil that determines the quality of fruit you will bear. So if your soil does not have any nutrients, then you shouldn't expect healthy fruit, or any fruit at all.

That is the same way offence works. It is poisonous to the soil of your heart. Anything you plant in poisonous soil will not bear fruit. If you want genuine wealth, tend the soil of your heart and refuse to hold on to bitterness.

Proverbs 4:23 (NLT)
Guard your heart above all else,
for it determines the course of your life.

Release Unforgiveness

It would be misleading if I tell you that
forgiveness is easy. We have all been hurt
before and we know how difficult it may be
to offer forgiveness in the face of so much
pain. Your faith can really be tested in the
face of hurt.

How I wish we could be exempt from
people hurting us but because we still live
in this fallen world, hurt is inevitable. So
how do you deal when someone or
something has caused you so much pain?
You let it go. Yes, you let it go because
holding on to unforgiveness hurts you more
than it hurts them.

Unforgiveness is like drinking poison and
expecting someone else to die for it.
People do not suffer because you're
holding them to unforgiveness in your
heart. On the contrary, most of them go
about their daily lives oblivious to the fact
that you haven't forgiven them.

When you live in unforgiveness, God can not work through you. You live in a self-made prison where you can get psychosomatic illnesses, you age quickly and just generally destroy yourself.

Whoever you're holding in your heart is not worth it. Let it go. It doesn't mean that you have to reconcile but release yourself from the prison of unforgiveness.

Matthew 18:21-22 (NLT)
Then Peter came to him and asked, "Lord, how often should I forgive someone who sins against me? Seven times?"
"No, not seven times," Jesus replied, "but seventy times seven!

Faith It Till You Make It

If you want all the conditions to be okay before you take the first step then you will remain a poor man. When you hear the voice of God, do not hesitate to move in obedience. When God says it and you do it then He blesses it, that is the mystery of faith.

No one ever amounts to anything tangible

or intangible in life without faith. The world calls it risk but we call it faith. You have to have faith to become something. Genuine wealth is built not by the tangible but by the intangible.

When you see it in the realm of the spirit, you can start to imagine it. Even if you don't own it physically yet, can you imagine yourself possessing wealth? If you can see it, God is committed to making it a reality.

Chapter 7

Work, Serve and Be Thankful

When learning about being successful or getting wealth, working will often be mentioned as one of the sure ways of being successful. Your work is a channel for blessings to come. What do you do? Are you actively involved in any wealth-creating activities?

We live in a generation where a lot of arrogant individuals assume that wealth will come to them on a platter of gold without having to put in any effort. People are consumed with the desire for wealth and fame but are not diligent enough to work for it. Yet again, others expect that just praying and saying amen to prophecies will make a difference without any responsibility from their side. Both of these extremes are far from the truth.

James 2:14, 26 (NLT)
What good is it, dear brothers and sisters, if

you say you have faith but don't show it by your actions? Can that kind of faith save anyone?
Just as the body is dead without breath, so also faith is dead without good works.

Scriptures say your faith achieves nothing if good works don't accompany it. You have to give God something to work with. In the Old Testament, God promised to bless the work of your hands. This means that if your hands don't work, then there is nothing for God to bless.

Let me tell you a story of a widow who had two sons. Her husband left her in debt when he passed on. The widow was going through a difficult time because her husband's debtors wanted to take her sons as slaves to pay for the debt. The woman went to Elisha for help, and Elisha asked her an important question:

2 Kings 4:2 (NLT)
Elisha replied to her, "How can I help you? Tell me, what do you have in your house?"
The woman said she had nothing except a small jar of oil.

I share this story because most people are like this woman; they think they have nothing and despise their small jar of oil. What is your small jar of oil? What is that gift, talent or business that you underestimate?

In this story, Elisha gave the widow instructions on what to do with her small jar of oil and the oil multiplied to the extent that she was able to pay off debt and have enough to live on from the proceeds of the oil sale.

What you have in your hand can be the key to your wealth and success. Resources are released to those who have something they're working on. Wealth comes to doers because God blesses the work of your hands, and whatsoever you DO prospers.

The life of a lazy man is a life of poverty. Only labourers are rewarded. If you aren't a labourer don't expect favour, and don't expect any reward. God doesn't like waste, He gives to people who are doing something.

You have to start from somewhere. Put your effort towards doing something productive and building your wealth from there. Do not despise little beginnings. Instead of complaining about the little income you earn from your business, invest in yourself and in your business so that you can grow. Learn from those that have gone ahead of you, take classes, ask questions and apply yourself. Before you know it the "little" business will grow into a major organization. Before you earn 6 figures, you may have to start with one figure.

Principles of a Successful Worker

Be a Hard Worker

Favour only follows labourers. To be successful you must work hard. You must be determined to give your all into the work of your hands. When you give your best, favour will follow you and God will bless the work of your hands.

1 Corinthians 15:10 (NLT)
But whatever I am now, it is all because God poured out his special favour on me—and not without results. For I have worked harder than any of the other apostles; yet it was not I but God who was working through me by his grace.

Work with Integrity

Can God trust you with His resources? Can He trust you with His people? You must live a life of integrity. In simple terms, integrity is who you are when no one is watching. If you want success in all that you do, you should make integrity one of your core values.

People do business with those they know, like and trust. If you are not trustworthy, you will lose clients, you will lose customers, you will lose helpers and worse of all, you will lose God's favour.

Psalm 41:11-12 (NLT)
I know that you are pleased with me,
for my enemy does not triumph over me.
Because of my integrity you uphold me
and set me in your presence forever.

Be a Diligent Worker

Diligence means being careful and persistent in your work. It means you set and commit to the right goals, you manage your time and resources well, you are efficient and are committed to continuous learning. This is what will cause you to stand before kings. Even a reasonable employer would reward such effort, how much more God!

Proverbs 22:29 (KJV)
Seest thou a man diligent in his business?
he shall stand before kings; he shall not
stand before mean men.

Work Skillfully and Creatively

With the rapid change in technology, improving your skills is a must. There is no excuse to not get better at what you are doing. Education and information are now available at the tip of your fingers. Make it a point of duty to be skilful by continuously learning and practicing what you have learnt. It is only applied knowledge that makes a difference.

Psalms 78:72 (NLT)
He cared for them with a true heart
and led them with skillful hands.

Be Relentless

Success does not come to those who quit and give up along the way. To be honest, the path to success is not linear and there are many ups and downs along the way. However, giving up is not an option if you truly want to achieve genuine wealth.

Embrace patience and perseverance throughout the journey, hold on to God's promises and trust in his faithfulness. It may seem like nothing is working out but if you persevere and relentlessly pursue your dream, all things will work together for your good and you will succeed!

Galatians 6:9 (NLT)
So let's not get tired of doing what is good. At just the right time we will reap a harvest of blessing if we don't give up.

Service and Gratitude

Beyond work, you must decide to always serve God's interest. Do not let your work or pursuits of wealth take you away from true service.

Serving God means looking out for his interests; which include the church, souls, his people and his creation. At the end of the day, when all is said and done, God will not ask you how much money you made while you were on earth. He will not ask you about the property you acquired or the career ladder you climbed. But He will ask you about the souls you impacted and the way you lived your life.

Matthew 25:34-40 (NLT)

*"Then the King will say to those on his right,
'Come, you who are blessed by my Father,
inherit the Kingdom prepared for you from
the creation of the world. For I was hungry,
and you fed me. I was thirsty, and you gave
me a drink. I was a stranger, and you invited
me into your home. I was naked, and you
gave me clothing. I was sick, and you cared
for me. I was in prison, and you visited me.'
"Then these righteous ones will reply, 'Lord,
when did we ever see you hungry and feed
you? Or thirsty and give you something to
drink? Or a stranger and show you
hospitality? Or naked and give you clothing?
When did we ever see you sick or in prison
and visit you?'
"And the King will say, 'I tell you the truth,
when you did it to one of the least of these
my brothers and sisters, you were doing it to
me!'*

As much as success and wealth are God's
will for your life, they should not take the
place of other important areas of your life.
Scriptures say in Matthew 6 that you should
seek God's kingdom above all else and
THEN everything else will be added to you.
His kingdom is a priority and your life must
reflect that.

Do not neglect fellowshipping with other believers, serving in church, or taking care of your family and the family of God at large just because you are searching for wealth. At the end of the day, heaven is the real goal and Jesus is our reward.

While on your journey, you will also do well to remember to maintain a posture of gratitude. It may be difficult and it may seem slow in coming, but still be grateful. You may have lost some things but be grateful that you haven't lost everything.

God can not and will not resist a grateful heart.

1 Thessalonians 5:16-18 (NLT)
Always be joyful. Never stop praying. Be thankful in all circumstances, for this is God's will for you who belong to Christ Jesus.

Chapter 8

Channels of Wealth

Now that we have discussed the basics of genuine wealth, we can go into detail on how we can create channels of wealth in our lives. There are two channels for wealth we will discuss in this chapter: spiritual channel and physical channel.

Channels are passages that allow a flow into or out of your life. Think of a pipe, for instance, for there to be a flow of water from one place to another, the pipe must be free from any blockages or hindrances. The pipe is the channel that allows the flow into or out of a place.

Similarly, you can create channels that allow a flow of wealth in and out of your life. These will be the ways in which you are watered and wealth has access to you. You must always maintain a flow in and out of you.

Most times we make the mistake of trying to hoard what we have. We selfishly think that hoarding is what will bring wealth. By all means, be wise with the way you deal with money but do not be a hoarder. Hoarding is similar to creating a blockage in the channel which cuts out the flow.

We can learn from our bodies; everything you eat gets in your body and is distributed according to the body's needs. Some are absorbed for immediate use, some are stored for later, some are invested into other body mechanisms, and some have to flow out of the body. If our bodies hoard all the food and there is no outflow, that will be a problem. For anything to function well there must be an inflow and an outflow.

Even in scripture, we see that God created Eden intentionally and allowed for a flow into and out of the garden. There was a river with four branches flowing into and out of Eden.

Genesis 2:10-14 (NLT)
A river flowed from the land of Eden, watering the garden and then dividing into four branches. The first branch, called the Pishon, flowed around the entire land of Havilah, where gold is found. The gold of that land is exceptionally pure; aromatic resin and onyx stone are also found there. The second branch, called the Gihon, flowed around the entire land of Cush. The third branch, called the Tigris, flowed east of the land of Asshur. The fourth branch is called the Euphrates.

Spiritual Channels

Every wealthy person has a combination of

the spiritual and physical. When I say spiritual, I don't only mean from God - people consult the devil for money too. The difference is that wealth from God's blessing doesn't come with sorrow. The enemy, on the other hand, deals with you selfishly and is only interested in stealing, killing and destroying you. Nothing from him comes without sorrow.

Money flows every day, it is either flowing to you or away from you. For it to flow to you, you must know what to do. There is a flow of money and wealth that could only come from God. When all you get is what you work for then you are yet to experience God's favour where money is concerned.

There are 4 spiritual channels that create wealth. If you create these channels, you are one step closer to becoming all that God has destined for you.

1. Tithing

Unfortunately, tithing has a bad reputation in many Christian communities. People associate tithing with theft, oppression of the poor and even fake pastors. Others go as far as refusing to be part of this important

biblical principle and slandering those who
do.

That is not at all what tithing is about. We do
not tithe because God needs your money,
He already owns everything. Tithing is a
biblical principle that teaches us to put God
first even in our finances. God does not
need your money, but He wants what your
money represents - your heart! Tithing is an
act of worship.

Matthew 6:21 (NLT)
Wherever your treasure is, there the desires
of your heart will also be.

Tithing is actually one of the surest ways of
crushing the spirit of poverty. Here are some
of the benefits of tithing

- Protection: As a tither, you are
  protected. When you obediently
  follow God's law, He is committed to
  ensuring that the benefits of your
  obedience are granted. The
  scriptures speak of this assurance in
  Isaiah 1:18-19 and 1 Corinthians
  10:13. Whatever challenges you
  may be facing, rest assured that
  others are going through similar

trials. God knows that you possess the strength and resilience to overcome them. It is important to remember that breaking a law often leads to our own undoing. God, therefore, values adherence to principles over mere prayers. While prayer remains significant, it is through living by godly principles that we truly honor Him. Additionally, when you give, you are under the protective covering of the Almighty.

- Preservation: God's divine design for those who faithfully tithe includes the preservation of their lineage. In Genesis 28:21-22, we learn that when we tithe, God safeguards us from the schemes of the enemy. Malachi 3:11 assures us that the fruits of our labour will not be destroyed. Through tithing, we are also shielded from shame and disgrace.

- Blessings: When you faithfully tithe, God delights in pouring out His blessings upon you (Malachi 3:10). Recognize that your tithe should extend beyond your income; even financial gifts and business earnings should be tithed. As a business owner, it is important to present the tithe from your business as well.

- Abundance of Rain: God sends abundant rain to tithers. Zechariah 10:1 and Joel 2:23-26 highlight the blessings that await tithers. When you commit to tithing, you will witness God's showers of blessings upon your life. His abundant provision will surprise and amaze you.

- Divine Provision and Care: Haggai 2:8-9 reminds us that as tithers, we can expect God's provision. Just as Canada's tax system offers breaks for those who give, our Heavenly Father also rewards our faithfulness. He ensures that our needs are met and cares for us in remarkable ways.

- Preparation for Tomorrow: In Genesis 32:24-30, we see the story of Jacob wrestling with God. Through this encounter, Jacob's life was transformed. Likewise, as tithers, we can expect God to prepare us for the future. He equips us with the necessary strength,

wisdom, and foresight to navigate
the challenges that lie ahead.

- A Plan for Prosperity: Tithers
  consistently receive divine ideas for
  prosperity. When we align ourselves
  with God's principles, He reveals
  strategies and opportunities that
  lead to success. Trust in His
  guidance and believe that He
  desires to bless you abundantly.

- Empowerment through God's Spirit:
  God provides tithers with power. As
  we faithfully give and live according
  to His principles, His Spirit
  empowers us to live victoriously. We
  can overcome obstacles, break free
  from limitations, and achieve great
  things with His strength.

- God's Ever-Present Company: The
  presence of God accompanies every
  tither. When we faithfully give, we
  enjoy a close relationship with Him.
  His guidance, comfort, and peace
  are with us every step of the way.

By embracing the practice of tithing, you
open yourself up to a world of divine
blessings and protection. Trust in God's

promises, faithfully give back to Him and experience the abundant life He desires for you.

Malachi 3:10 (NLT)
Bring all the tithes into the storehouse so there will be enough food in my Temple. If you do," says the LORD of Heaven's Armies, "I will open the windows of heaven for you. I will pour out a blessing so great you won't have enough room to take it in! Try it! Put me to the test!

2. First Fruit

Giving your first fruit is another spiritual channel that brings wealth. Your first fruit is the best of what God gives you. For example, when you get a new job or at the beginning of the year, you give God your first income to signify giving Him your first and your best.

Proverbs 3:9-10 (NLT)
*Honour the LORD with your wealth and with the best part of everything you produce.
Then he will fill your barns with grain,*

and your vats will overflow with good wine.

3. Kingdom Development and Building

It goes without saying that when you take care of God's business, He will take care of you. Be committed to giving to build his kingdom by supporting kingdom activities like missions, giving to orphans and widows, and giving towards any need in your local assembly as much as you are able to.

4. Offering

Giving your offering is one of the ways to ensure fruitfulness in your life. Give your offering to God in your local assembly, give to family members and to the family of God at large. When God blesses you with an income, it isn't meant for you alone. Do your best to give to the family of God whenever you are able to.

Proverbs 11:24-25 (NLT)

Give freely and become more wealthy;
be stingy and lose everything.
The generous will prosper;
those who refresh others will
themselves be refreshed

Physical Channels

Just like we had spiritual channels, we also have physical channels if you want to create wealth. Here are four physical channels on your journey to building a wealthy and successful life.

1. Do Business

The concept of "doing business" is not new. It has existed even as far back as biblical times. We see multiple examples of bible characters who were business owners. Peter was a fisherman, Paul was a tent maker, Lydia was a merchant of expensive purple, Abraham's business was in agriculture and cattle rearing...the list goes on.

As we can see, doing business is one of the ways to build wealth.

Luke 19:13 (NKJV)
So he called ten of his servants, delivered to them ten minas, and said to them, 'Do business till I come.'

Each of us has something to sell or offer. God has placed within us the potential for productivity and growth. Whatever we have in our hands has the capacity to reproduce and generate blessings. We cannot truly occupy until we have a business or a venture that aligns with God's purpose for our lives.

Using the story of the widow's oil again (2 Kings 4:1-7), we have to have something in our hand that God will use to multiply. The widow experienced God's unique movement in her life and her children's life because of the business she had selling oil. At first, she underestimated the oil she had, but because God breathed on it, her oil business not only cleared her debts but also provided her with extra to live on. The proceeds of her business offered security for herself and her children.

By embracing the principles of business and stewarding the resources God has entrusted to you, you position yourself to create generational wealth that leaves an inheritance even for your descendants. Being solely dependent on employment limits your ability to build wealth and pass it on to the next generation.

2. Invest

Let us delve into the concept of investment, specifically the investment of honour. Honour is an investment that yields multiple returns. To honour someone is to recognize their inherent value as beings made in the image of God.

1 Peter 2:17 (NKJV)
Honour all people. Love the brotherhood. Fear God. Honour the king.

But before we discuss honour, let us learn from Noah, the first recorded investor in the Bible. After emerging from the ark, Noah started to plant. Before that, no one had ever planted before. Noah took a risk when he planted. This act of planting symbolized the beginning of the first law of sowing and reaping, with Noah being the pioneer of investment.

Ecclesiastes 11:1-2 (NLT)
Send your grain across the seas,
and in time, profits will flow back to you.
But divide your investments among many
places,
for you do not know what risks might lie
ahead.

Investments are risky. Whether you invest your money, your emotions or even investments in people. There is a possibility of loss but there is also a possibility of great gain. The fear of loss should not be your guiding principle when investing.

In this day and age ignorance is not an excuse. You can learn the basics of investing online and even go beyond the basics to learn everything you can. Commit to investing and being a good steward of the resources God has given you. There will come a time when God will make a demand on what He has given to you.

Now, let us discuss the investment of honour. Every person on earth is a seed, planted by God and also a seed from our parents. This is why even God requires us to bear fruit. He expects a return on investments.

As seeds from our parents, our lives have the potential to bring blessings if we honour them. Honouring our parents, pastors, elders, leaders and authority figures in our lives and acknowledging the investments they have made in our lives can unlock a new level of wealth and prosperity. By understanding the importance of honour we position ourselves to receive a return on investment.

3. Love

There is an inseparable connection between love and giving. True love cannot exist without giving. While it is possible to give without genuinely loving, you can't truly love without giving, and without love there can never be true wealth.

True love requires a mindset that places the needs and desires of others above your own. It is more blessed to give than to receive therefore, you must go beyond thinking of yourself and considering the well-being of others.

Philippians 4:19 (NKJV)
And my God shall supply all your need according to His riches in glory by Christ Jesus.

We usually like to quote this verse when praying over our finances but do you know the context of this scripture? When you read further back you see that Paul prayed this over the Philippian church because of their generous financial gift to him. The church there was the only one that cared enough about his well-being that they sent financial help. That is true love.

Genuine goodness is demonstrated through

acts of love and generosity toward others. By embracing the principle of giving as an expression of true love, you position yourself to receive the abundant blessings and wealth that flow from a heart that gives unconditionally.

4. Understand Wealth in Your Country

In this final physical channel of wealth, we will focus on practical advice on understanding and navigating the pathways to wealth within the specific context of a given country. Take Canada for example, which is my current country of residence, I will highlight several key factors that contribute to wealth accumulation.

- Taxes: I can't overemphasize the importance of understanding the tax system. A comprehensive grasp of tax laws and regulations enables you to optimize your financial resources and minimize tax liabilities, which creates a favourable environment for wealth creation. In Canada, businesses and individuals who understand the tax system reap the benefits financially. Do you know how taxes work in your country? Reach out to a tax professional and get educated. It is impossible to beat a system you don't understand.

- Life Insurance, Wills and Estate Planning: Death is a topic that many would rather avoid. I understand that it can be disturbing to think about the loss of a loved one or the loss of your life but many problems come up when a breadwinner or someone in the family passes away.

  We have heard stories of families whose lives were changed for the worst after losing the breadwinner. Sometimes it is the funeral expenses that burden the family. Even today we see a lot of gofundme campaigns going on to support funeral arrangements. Part of building wealth is making a plan for when you are no longer here. Ensure that you have written a will and you have a life insurance policy in case of anything. Lighten the burden on your family by preparing for unforeseen events.

Proverbs 13:22 (NKJV)

*A good man leaves an inheritance to
his children's children*

- Education Savings Plans and
  Pension Plans: These are financial
  instruments that provide avenues for
  long-term wealth accumulation and
  retirement security. In Canada, we
  have RESP which is a Registered
  Education Savings Plan where you
  can put money away towards your
  children's education. You can start
  as early as possible and the
  government will also contribute
  towards it. That is a great way of
  building funds and planning ahead
  so that your children can go to
  school stress-free. You also won't
  have to worry about where tuition
  will come from because you have
  prepared in advance.

  Similarly, there are pension plans
  that allow you to invest towards your
  retirement. I would advise that you
  have a personal pension plan in
  addition to anything you will receive
  from the government and any plan
  your employer offers. Some
  employers also offer a matching
  contribution towards your pension

plan, if you can, take advantage of that free money your employer gives.

- Real Estate: This is a powerful tool for wealth creation. Understanding the dynamics of the real estate market, property investment, and related strategies empowers individuals to leverage this asset class to generate wealth and financial stability.

The Time is Now

As the saying goes, the best time to plant a tree was yesterday, the next best time is today. It's never too late to start applying the principles you have learned from this book. In fact, there is no better time to start pursuing your dreams and living the life you desire than today.

Everything you need to obtain genuine wealth is already in you. God has a purpose for your life and has equipped you and surrounded you with all you need to achieve it. His plan will lead you to a prosperous and hopeful future. I urge you to get started, but more importantly, I urge you to go with God.

I pray that the words you have read in this book will inspire you to take action because knowledge without action is knowledge wasted, but knowledge that is acted upon is wisdom! I pray that God will be glorified through your wealth. Finally, I am rooting for you and I can't wait to hear your testimonies.

www.ingramcontent.com/pod-product-compliance
Lightning Source LLC
Chambersburg PA
CBHW071742200326
41519CB00021BC/6829